Five-Minute art IDEAS print

Edited by
Nicola Wright

Designed and illustrated by
Chris Dymond

Contents

Ideals Children's Books • Nashville, Tennessee
an imprint of Hambleton-Hill Publishing, Inc.

Hints and Tips

Before you begin making any of the ideas in this book, put on old clothes so that it won't matter if you get messy.

Keep some scrap paper handy for trying out your prints before you use your good paper.

Cover your work area with old newspapers before you start in case anything spills.

Always ask an adult to help when using sharp objects such as craft knives. You can buy round-ended safety scissors from most craft shops.

There are many different types of paint you can use to make your prints. Poster paint is one of the best.

It is a good idea to keep pieces of scrap paper, cloth, and other bits and pieces you have collected in a box. Then they will be ready to use when you need them.

There are lots of different types of glue that can be used to stick objects to blocks or cardboard so you can print with them. A craft glue is one of the best to use, unless the directions say otherwise.

Remember to rinse your brushes after using them and to clean up afterward!

Handy Prints

You need

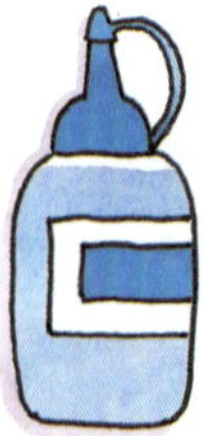
Liquid paint

Scissors

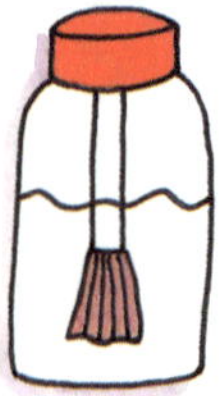
Glue

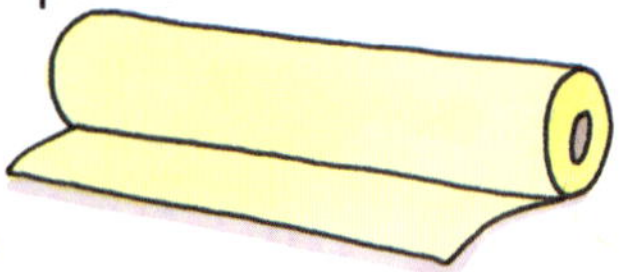
Craft paper

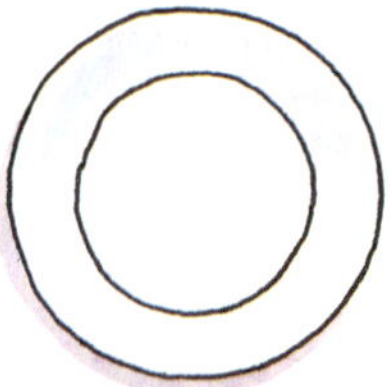
Plate

1

Pour some paint on a plate. Place your hand in the paint, and then press your hand down on the craft paper.

2

Make lots of hand prints in different colors.

3

When the paint is dry, cut around each hand shape.

Add details such as eyes and mouths to bring the picture to life.

Make a long wildlife picture for your bedroom wall.

Top tip

Get your friends to help make different sizes of hand prints.

Cut out hand prints and stick them on fabric for fancy dress costumes.

4

Layer your prints to make birds, trees, animals, and fish.

Layer the prints to form a picture on another sheet of craft paper. Glue them in place.

String Prints

You need

Draw a simple picture on thick cardboard. Cover the cardboard with glue and outline your drawing with string. Wait for the glue to dry.

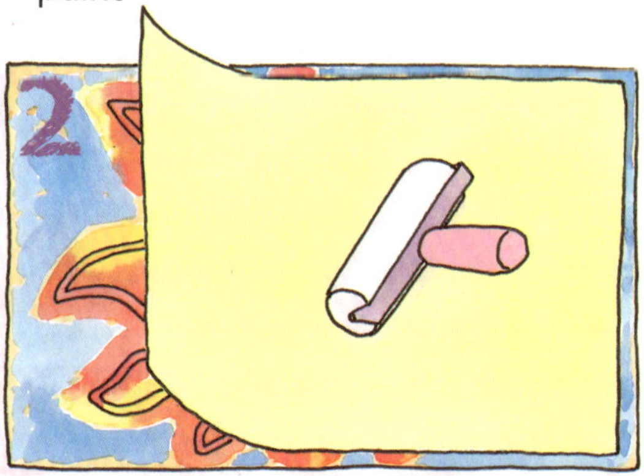

Brush paint thinly and evenly onto the string. Lay paper over the top and roll over the back of it with an ink roller. Peel the paper back carefully.

Instead of an ink roller, you could use a rolling pin or soda bottle.

1

For another kind of print, cut two 4-inch (10-cm) squares from the cardboard. Make marks every 1/2 inch (1 cm) down the sides. Draw wavy lines to link the dots.

2

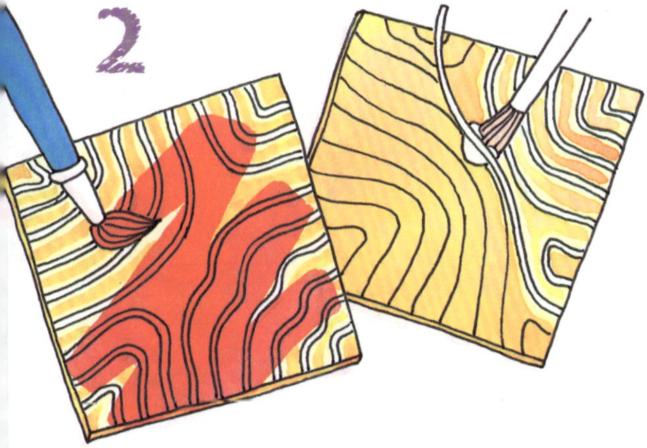

Glue string over the lines. Let it dry, and cover with paint as before.

Use your printed paper for wrapping gifts. Make a card and gift tag to match.

3

Press one square down in a corner of a sheet of paper. Line the other square up to the first and print again. Then print the first one again, and so on, until the sheet is covered.

Odds and Ends

You need

Everyday objects from around the house

Liquid paint

Paper

Plates

1

Find small objects around the house that have interesting shapes and flat surfaces. Ask an adult if the objects you have chosen are all right to use.

2

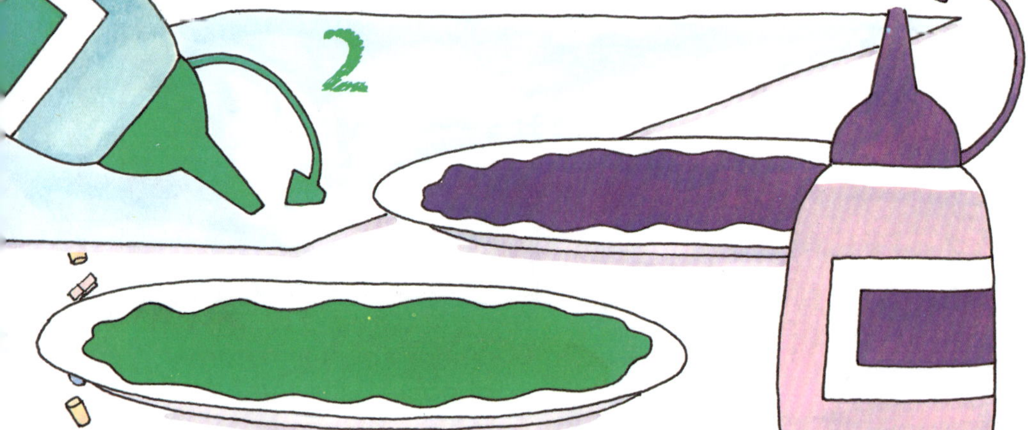

Put some different colors of paint into plates.

3

Dip your object into the paint and then press it down firmly on a sheet of paper. Build up a pattern by using different shapes and colors.

Top tip

If the objects you use are needed again, use a water-base paint that can be washed off.

Sticky Prints

You need

Smooth, wipeable surface

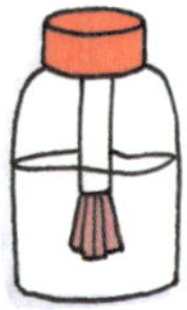

Thick paste glue

Powdered paint

Newspaper

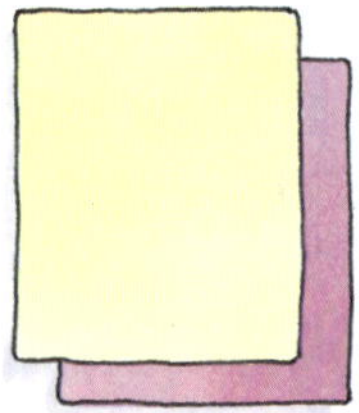

Paper

1

Put one color of paint on one side of the glue and another color on the other side for a multicolor print.

Place a dollop of glue in the center of a smooth, wipeable surface. Add a small spoonful of powdered paint to the glue.

2 Mix together the powdered paint and glue with your finger. Spread the mixture thinly over the surface.

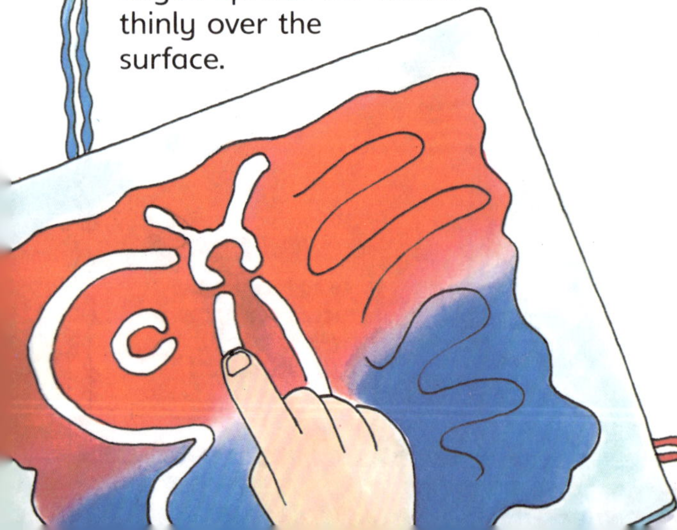

3 Draw a pattern or shape in the mixture, using thick, wide lines. Place a sheet of paper over it. Then lay a piece of newspaper over the top.

Press the newspaper down hard, smoothing across the whole surface.

Remove the newspaper and then carefully peel off the paper, starting at one corner. Let it dry.

Top tip

Make a pattern, such as water, to use as a background. Then glue an animal or other shape on top to make a picture.

If you draw a shape in the glue, you can cut it out and stick it on top of a pattern.

Veggie Prints

You need

2

Put different colors of paint in plates. Dip the pieces of fruit and vegetables in the paint.

1

Ask an adult to cut up the fruit and vegetables for you. Try cutting different shapes into them.

Top tip

After dipping the piece of fruit or vegetable into paint, press it down on a piece of scrap paper before you print with it. This will get rid of any extra paint and give you a better print.

You can now use these pieces to print interesting patterns or pictures on your paper.

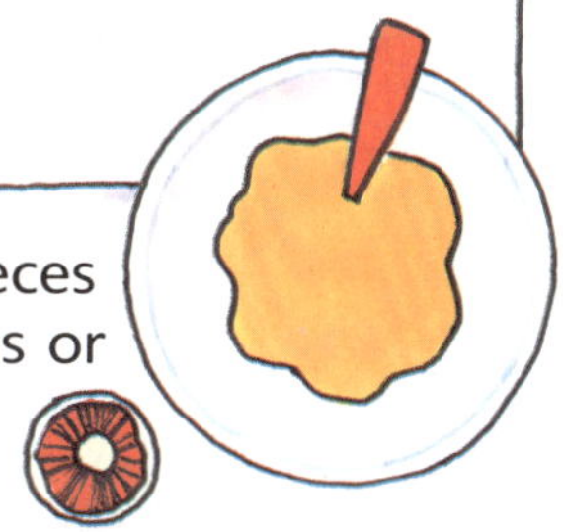

Rag Printing

You need

Printing with the closed or the open end of the rag will give you different effects.

1 Twist and scrunch up a rag. Wrap a rubber band around it tightly to hold the shape together.

2 Put some paint in a plate. Dip the end of the rag into the paint and lightly dab it over a sheet of paper.

Use other rags to print with different colors.

When the paint is dry, turn the paper over and draw shapes. Cut them out and stick them together to make pictures.

Block Printing

You need

White paint on colored paper looks good.

1 Look around the house for interesting objects with which to print. Glue them onto a block in a pattern. Wait for the glue to dry.

2 Pour some paint in a plate. Press the patterned side of the block into the paint and then onto paper.

Top tip

Press objects into a block of clay and then remove. Press the block into paint and then onto paper. The shape of the object will show up as white.

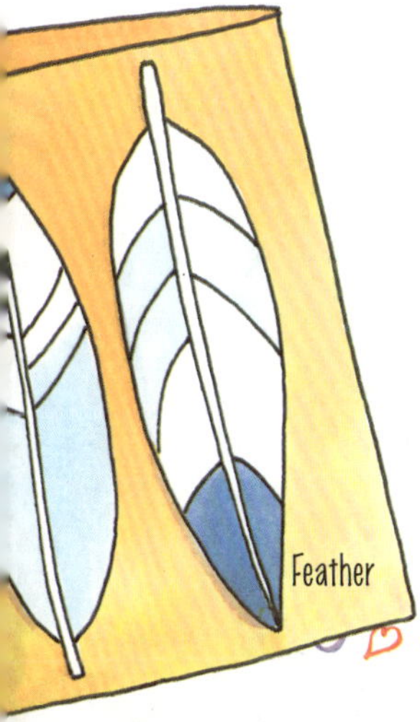

Marbling

You need

1

Fill a baking pan almost to the rim with water. Add a few drops of vinegar to the water.

2 Now mix your paint with some turpentine to make it thin and drop small amounts of different colored paints into the water.

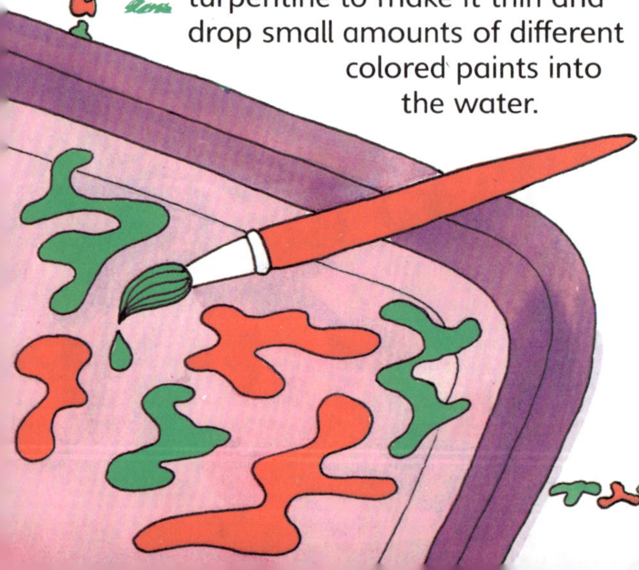

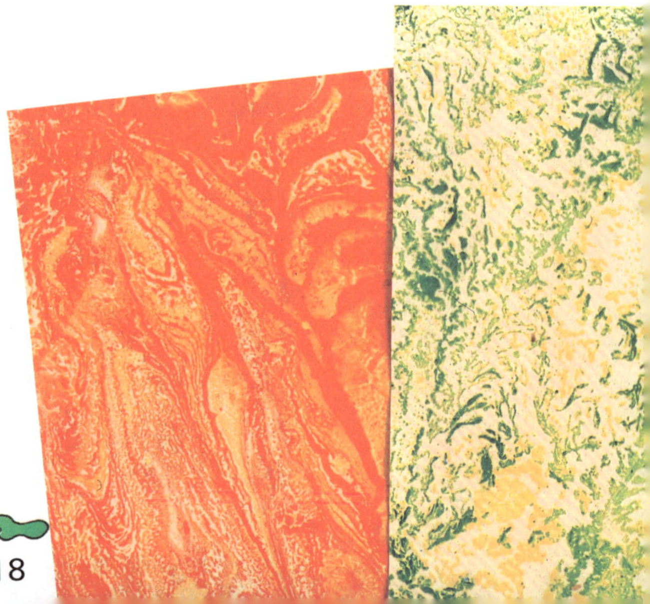

3

Lay a sheet of paper on the water. Wait a couple of seconds and then lift it off.

4 Let the paper dry and you will see your marbled effect.

Use the paper to wrap gifts, or cut shapes out of it and stick them on poster board to make pictures.

Top tip

If you put wallpaper paste into the water as well as vinegar, your pattern will set even better.

Rolling Pin

You need

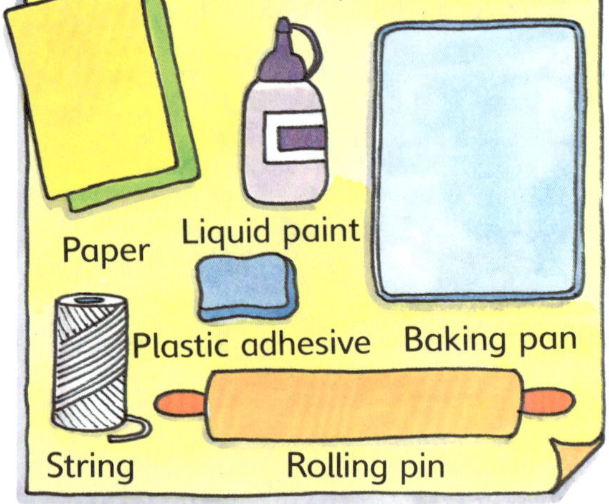

1 Tie a piece of string to one end of a rolling pin or cardboard tube. Wind the string tightly around it until you reach the other end and tie the string again.

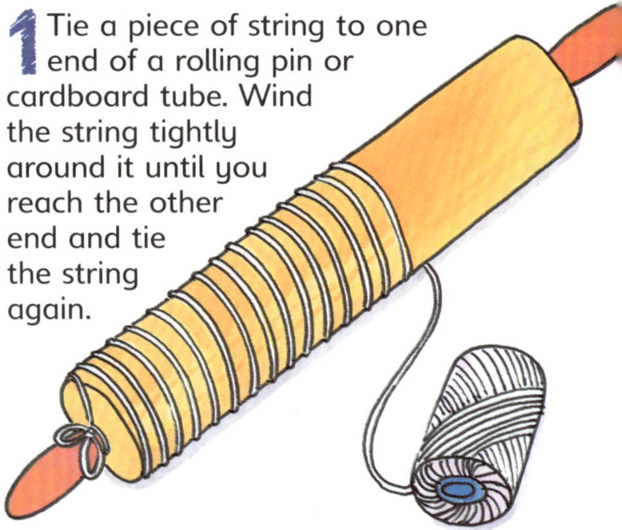

2 Tear or cut shapes out of paper. Stick the shapes on a piece of paper with a little plastic adhesive.

3

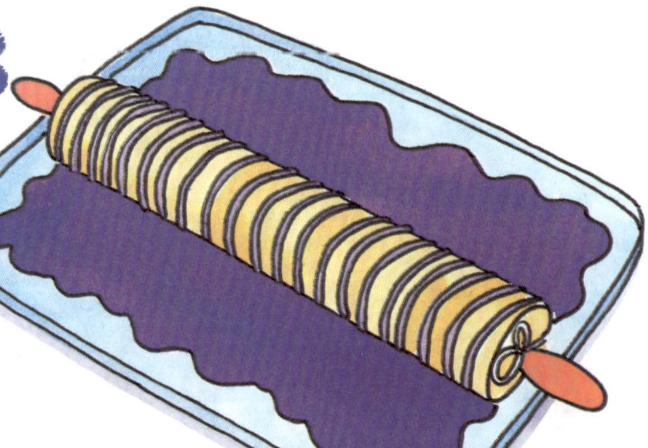

Place paint in a baking pan. Roll pin in paint until all the string is covered.

You can do lots of different things using the rolling pin. Paint a tiger, leaving out the stripes. Then go over it with the rolling pin and it will look like a tiger in long grass.

4

Roll over the paper and the shapes. When the paint is dry, peel off the shapes.

Roll over the shapes again in a different direction to create a checked pattern.

Use the shapes to make pictures.

Pizza Prints

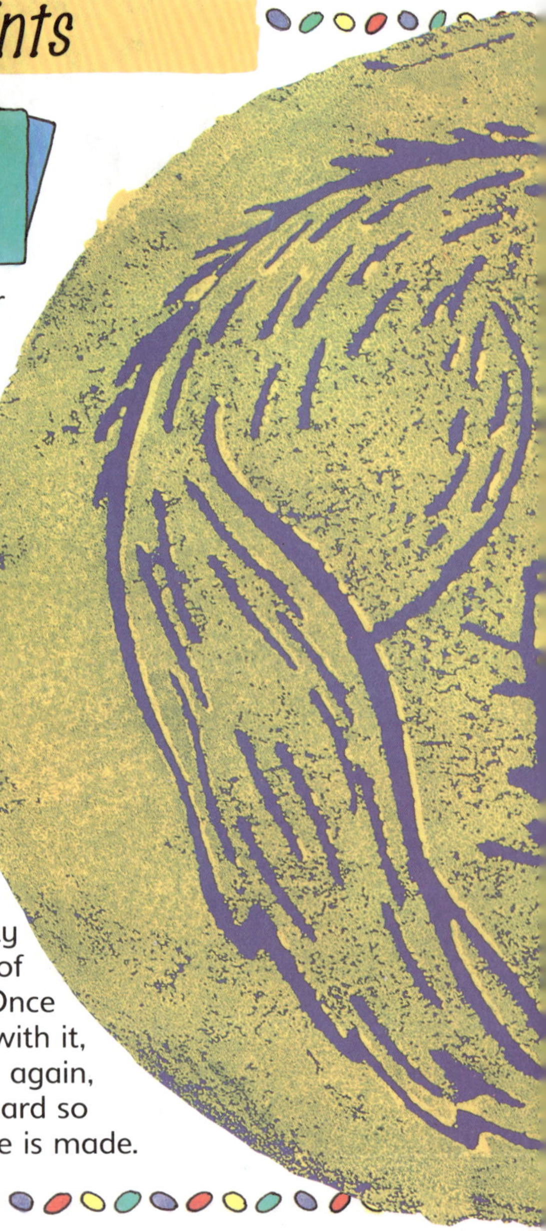

You need

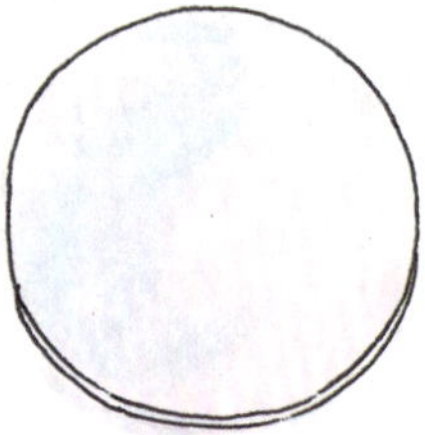

Sheet of polystyrene (for example, a pizza base)

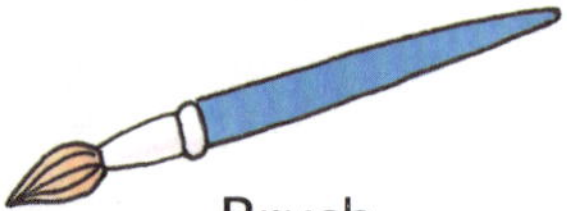

Brush

Paper

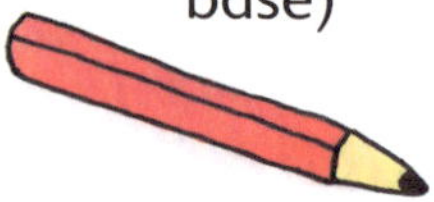

Pencil

Liquid paint

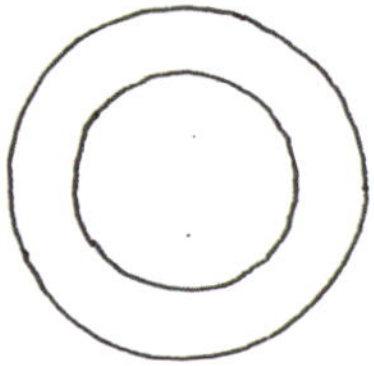

Plate

1

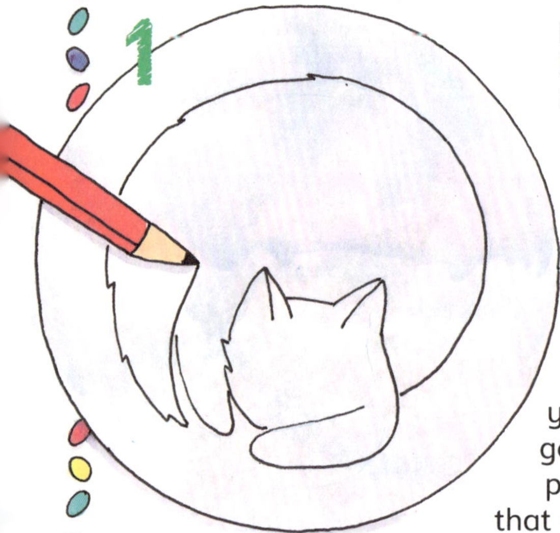

Draw deeper lines for your main outline.

Draw a shape lightly on a sheet of polystyrene. Once you are happy with it, go over the lines again, pressing down hard so that an indented line is made.

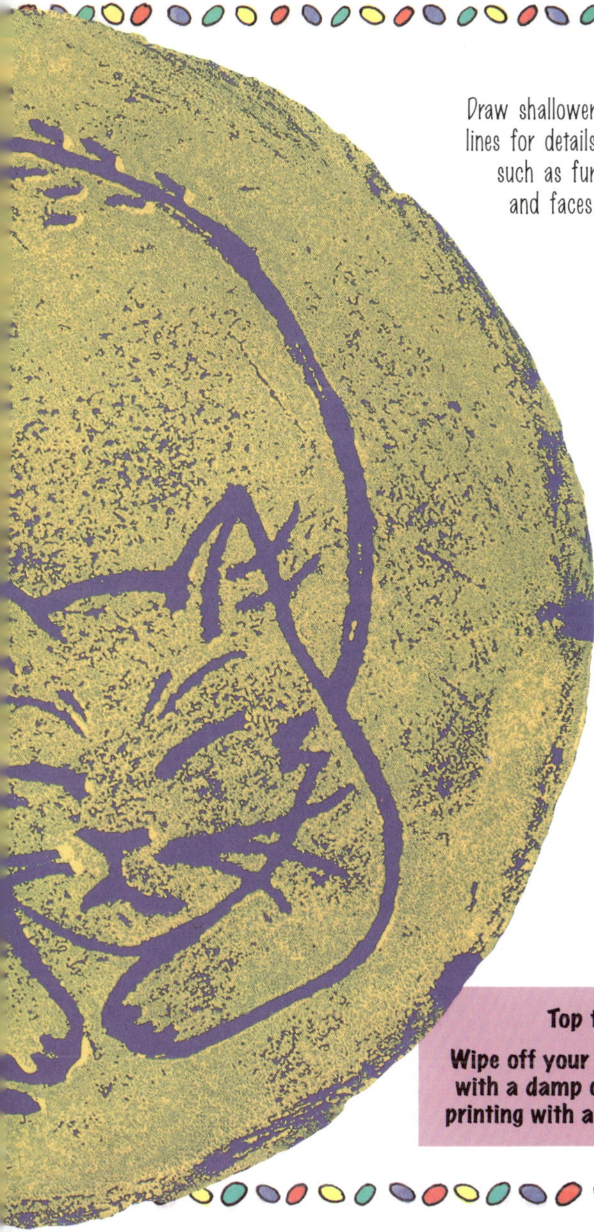

Draw shallower lines for details such as fur and faces.

2

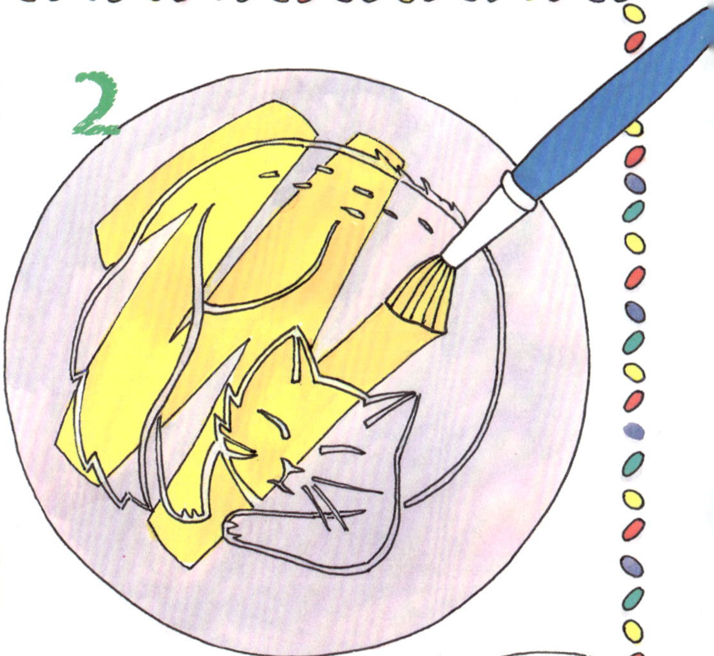

Quickly paint over the whole surface and then press it facedown on a sheet of paper.

Don't use too much paint and try not to get it in the lines.

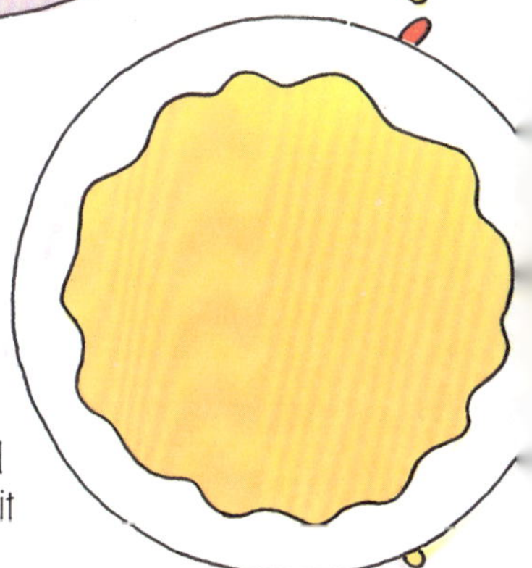

Top tip

Wipe off your polystyrene with a damp cloth before printing with another color.

More Ideas

Use your thumbs and fingers to create different pictures.

You need an ink stamp pad.

Complete your picture by adding details with a pen.

First published in the U.S. in 1995 by Ideals Children's Books
An imprint of Hambleton-Hill Publishing, Inc.
Nashville, Tennessee 37218

Produced by Zigzag Publishing Ltd., West Sussex, England.

Printed and bound in Hong Kong

ISBN 1-57102-059-4 (package)
ISBN 1-57102-059-4BK (book)